MUST TRY HARDER!

MUST TRY HARDER!

The Very Worst Howlers by Schoolchildren

Norman McGreevy

CONSTABLE • LONDON

Constable & Robinson Ltd
3 The Lanchesters
162 Fulham Palace Road
London W6 9ER
www.constablerobinson.com

First published in Australia by Allen & Unwin, 2006

First published in the UK by Constable,
an imprint of Constable & Robinson Ltd, 2007

A copy of the British Library Cataloguing in
Publication Data is available from the British Library

ISBN: 978-1-84529-632-2

Printed and bound in the EU

9 10 8

CONTENTS

Dear Reader,

If you have picked up this book then I trust we are kindred spirits, bound together by our collective outrage at the ways in which the youth of today are mangling the English language; chewing up words and spitting them out until, like a cashmere cardigan after it's been through the spin cycle, their beauty and power are diminished.

Be warned, your complicity in reading this book may see you accused of pedantry. Perhaps even cruelty. Old fashioned fuddy-duddiness. Be brave in the face of such taunts. I for one am proud to be a curmudgeon. I never vote for anyone. I vote against. I believe we have to save the earth from evangelical environmentalists and dubious politicians who like bananas start off green, turn yellow and then become rotten.

Nothing on TV, except documentaries about the eating habits of the common earwig, even remotely interests me, health food makes me sick, my favourite animal is bacon and the sight of any actor spouting serious opinions, on any topic, I find so completely laughable I have to go and lie down.

And so it is with curmudgeonly pride that I say we must stand united in our righteous protection of literary correctness. For if we allow this state of affairs to continue we will lose not only our future but our past.

It is outrageous, for example, that little Norman in 5G should think that 'Germany's William the Second had a chimp on his shoulder and therefore had to ride his horse with one hand' or that Catherine in 6A should truly believe 'Joan of Arc was Noah's sister'. This sort of thing, although inadvertently and deeply humorous, can not go unchecked.

And then there is the smut. When asked what he did in his summer holidays, Jack wrote: 'While rowing up river I slumped over the whores in a state of physical exhaustion'. This boy is not yet even out of long shorts.

I blame the well known fact that students can't read, write or spell on an education system where sharing feelings is more important than learning to achieve. A fellow curmudgeon I know likes to say that reading most of his student's English essays feels like watching somebody use a Stradivarius to pound nails. I couldn't agree more. In fact I only wish I'd said it myself.

I also blame television, of course. The influence of soap operas and movie gangsters is apparent in students' use of informal language in their essays, referring to Charles V as 'Philip's dad' or reporting that Luther had 'bad-mouthed' the Pope and the Gestapo 'did over' those who 'bad-mouthed' Hitler, they say.

But it doesn't stop there. What about this new fangled business of text messaging. Cul8r. Do these children read anything that isn't on a screen? Is it any wonder Mary thinks 'the appendix is a part of a book for which nobody ever found a use'?

I can offer only one consolation to soothe the blisters of our torment. Humour. The only good that can come of the murder of proper English language usage is laughter. And you will laugh my friends.

This leads me to one of the problems with the collection of howlers you hold in your hand. The reader may be tempted to read too many of them at one sitting. This is a mistake. It can be done, but it leaves the reader limp with laughter, much like over exercising, and it's really not worth doing, just for the sake of saying you have done it. Take it easy. Spread it out over the course of a week. Assimilate the benefits little by little. I'd recommend carrying it with you, dipping into it, and turning down the page corners, for a quick pick me up.

While I am sure many of the howlers in this collection have been cut and polished over the years, and many may doubt the authenticity of some of the more fanciful, there has been no need for invention. Indeed, any attempt at invention, soon stands out from their natural and uncontrived feel. There is a great feeling of satisfaction to know that you have produced a book that is guaranteed to bring laughter and amusement, and now even better health, to so many people. This compilation, *Must Try Harder!*, drawn from many thousands of howlers in exam papers and student essays, takes the very best to show that this well established tradition is very much alive and well. As for the preservation of the fine traditions of correct punctuation, sentence structure and factual accuracy, we can only hope and pray for a turnaround in this alarming trend towards casual and sloppy language.

As you start out on your crusade, fear not the cries of the unrighteous – 'Why are you always such a terrible curmudgeon; go out and have some fun; get a life' or more pointedly 'Shut up, and don't ever come to my house again, you miserable old bastard'. Forgive them, for they know not what they do. Ignoramuses.

Norman McGreevy
September 2006

School
Days

He closed his eyes in a gesture
of despair; he contorted his face,
praying for strength, and then
lifted his leg, aiming towards
the horizon.

He was a man of about
35 years of age, looked twenty
and was forty.

II

Pails and bowels were
flung all over the plaice.

Walking along the country lane,
with my feet in the stirrups.

The dream in every newlywed
couple's head is to marry.

If he is not checked at the right
age he will gradually develop
into a vandal, and it will not be
long before he is a magistrate.

If a tree falls in the dessert,
does it make a sound?

All the crew were taken
into custardy.

Upstairs, on the front of
the house, is the bathroom.
This comprises of one bath,
sink unit and toilet with enough
room to tuck one's toes in.

People were running all over
the place, the boys in shorts and
the girls in hysterics.

We had a longer holiday
than usual this year because
the school was closed
for altercations.

Girls were typically sent to
finishing school where the
point was to finish them off.

A hostage is a lady
who entertains visitors.

All teachers at our school
are certified.

A polygon is a man
who has many wives.

The headmaster caned me
only on rear occasions.

Writing of the school's old boys
in an essay on the war:
Those that did not go to the war
married, but the stronger ones
started a football team.

Our school is ventilated
by hot currants.

A school teacher leads
a sedimentary life.

Books & Words
& Stuff

A fairy tale is something that never happened a long time ago.

She worked herself up into an inarticulate comma.

Lady Jane Grey said she was content with her books, so she was beheaded.

The word trousers is an
uncommon noun because
it is singular at the top and
plural at the bottom.

The appendix is a part
of a book for which nobody
ever found a use.

Ovid wrote a poem called
the 'Medea' which was
lost fortunately.

Writing at the same time
as Shakespeare was
Miguel Cervantes. He was
Donkey Hote.

Polonius was a mythical sausage.

Shakespeare married Anne Hathaway, but he mostly lived at Windsor with his merry wives. This is quite usual with actors.

Achilles appears in 'The Illiad', by Homer. Homer also wrote the 'Oddity', in which Penelope was the last hardship that Ulysses endured on his journey.

Homer wrote the Oddity. Actually, Homer was not written by Homer but by another man of that name.

Voltaire invented electricity and also wrote a book called 'Candy'.

John Milton wrote 'Paradise Lost'. Then his wife died and he wrote 'Paradise Regained'.

An epitaph is a short
sarcastic poem.

Poetry is when every line starts
with a capital letter and doesn't
reach the right side of the page.

Lord Byron wrote epics and swam
the Hellespont. In between he
made love drastically.

In Ibsen's Ghosts, Oswald dies
of congenial syphilis.

The brave knight was
swallowed up by the awful
abbess that yawned all of a
sudden in front of him.

Shakespeare lived in Windsor
with his merry wives, writing
tragedies, comedies and errors.

A relative pronoun is a
family pronoun, such as
'mother,' 'brother,' 'uncle'.

Letters in sloping type
are in hysterics.

Emphasis in reading is
putting more distress in one
place than another.

An abstract noun is one that
cannot be heard, seen,
touched, or smelt.

Brutus was a tragic hero in spite
of dying in the end.

In conclusion we may say that
Shylock was greedy, malicious,
and indeed, entirely viscous.

Geography

A consonant is a large piece of
land surrounded by water.

A glazier is a man who runs
down mountains.

The general direction of the
Alps is straight up.

The Wholey Roman Empire
amazed many when it was
found in Germany.

The population of Sydney
is a bit too thick.

Geography

A consonant is a large piece of
land surrounded by water.

A glazier is a man who runs
down mountains.

The general direction of the
Alps is straight up.

The climate of the island
is wet but embracing.

A Native American calls his
wife a squaw and his children
squawkers.

History

King Arthur lived in the
Age of Shivery.

My favorite myth was Jason
and the Huguenots.

Socrates died from an
overdose of wedlock.

In the Olympic games, Greeks ran races, jumped, hurled the biscuits, and threw the java.

The Persians outnumbered the Greeks because they had more men.

The wife of a duke is a dukky.

Helen of Troy launched a
thousand ships with her face.

Alexander the Great conquered
Persia, Egypt and Japan. Sadly
he died with no hairs.

Another Greek myth was Jason
and the Golden Fleas.

The Epicureans and the
Synthetics believed 'If you can't
play with it, why bother?'

Joan of Arc was burnt
to a steak.

Queen Elizabeth never married,
she had a peaceful reign.

Magna Carta provided that
no man should be hanged twice
for the same offence.

Joan of Arc was
Noah's sister.

When Elizabeth exposed herself
before her troops, they all
shouted, 'hurrah.'
Then her navy went out and
defeated the Spanish Armadillo.

Medieval people were violent.
Murder during this period
was nothing. Everybody
killed somebody.

During the Middle Ages
the Surfs were dentured
and bonded to the ground.

Two hundred years of rule by
the Tarts explains why Russia
became so backward.

The Turks manicured
the pilgrims.

Victims of the Black Death
grew boobs on their necks.

The King wore a scarlet robe
trimmed with vermin.

Ivan the Terrible started life
as a child, a fact that troubled
his later personality.

Arrested witches were torchured
until they told a story. The worst
of this could be the rack or
burning with hot porkers. Some
women were made to endure
the ducking stool.

In the middle of the 18th
century, all the morons
moved to Utah.

The German Emperor's lower
passage was blocked by
the English.

The War of the Spanish
Succession ended in a drawl.

The British used mostly Aztec
troops to do their fighting
at Gallipoli.

Germany's William the Second
had a chimp on his shoulder
and therefore had to ride his
horse with one hand.

In 1937 Lenin revolted Russia
after the Germans sent him
home in a soiled train.

Clive committed suicide three
times and the third time they
sent him to India.

Louis XVI was gelatined to death.

The French Revolution was
caused by overcharging taxis.

Henry VIII by his own efforts
increased the population of
England by 40 000.

Hitler's instrumentality of terror was the Gespacho.

When things didn't go as planned, Stalin used the peasants as escape goats.

Hitler committed suicide in his bunk.

Politics

When Caesar was assassinated,
he is reported to have said
'Me too, Brutus!'

King John ground the people
down under heavy taxis.

Karl Marx's Communist Fiesta
was very important.

Machiavelli who was often
unemployed, wrote 'The Prince'
to get a job with Richard Nixon.

Laissez-faire meant
'let the farmers pay the taxes'.

A caucus is a sort of big parrot
that has been taught to swear.

President Carter faced the
'Iran Hostess Crisis'.

The USSR and the USA became
global in power, but Europe
remained incontinent.

When Gorbachev became top
Russian the USSR shifted to a
new planet of existance.

Animals

Sharks were infesting the area,
and one of them was
a non-swimmer.

A Mayor is a he horse.

Benjamin Franklin discovered
electricity by rubbing two cats
backwards and declared,
'A horse divided against
itself cannot stand'.

An armadillo is an
ornamental shrub.

To keep milk from turning sour:
Keep it in the cow.

Marsupials are
poached animals.

The home of the swallow
is the stomach.

Anthroapologists have proved
that when animals were not
available the people ate
nuts and barrys.

Herrings go about
the sea in shawls.

A monkey has a
reprehensible tail.

Frogs have webbed feet for
swimming but, like ducks,
these are fine to walk on.

Men are mammals and
women are femammals.

The hydra gets its food by
descending upon its prey and
pushing it into its mouth
with its testicles.

The adder is a poisonous snack.

An octogenarian is an animal
which has eight young at birth.

One horsepower is the amount
of energy it takes to drag a horse
500 feet in one second.

The largest mammals are to be
found in the sea because there is
nowhere else to put them.

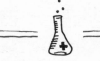

Science & Medicine

Some of the patients were plastered, and some were hanging from the ceiling.

For fractures: to see if the limb is broken, wiggle it gently back and forth.

For snakebites: bleed the wound and rape the victim in a blanket for shock.

If anyone should faint put her
head between the knees of the
nearest medical man.

Later on the doctor gave him
piles to relief him his pain.

Although the patient had
never been fatally ill before,
he woke up dead.

A circle is a figure with 0
corners and only one side.

A phlegmatic person is one who
has chronic bronchitis.

The liver is an infernal organ.

Nuclear activity causes
distortions in the jeans of women.

A city purifies its water supply by filtering the water and forcing it through an aviator.

A major discovery was made by Mary Leaky, who found a circle of rocks that broke wind.

Nets are holes surrounded by pieces of string.

Crude oil is a vicious substance.

The Scientific Revolution developed a suppository of knowledge which greatly helped later generations.

If you cross XY and XX chromosones, you get XX (female), YY (male) and XY (undecided).

An advantage of an organism having both sexual and asexual reproduction in its life-cycle: twice as much reproducing.

Al Chemy was a man who discovered chemistry.

If teeth are not cleaned, plague is the result.

Vacuums are nothings. We only
mention them to let them know
we know they are there.

In biology today,
we digested a frog.

To germinate is to become
a naturalised German.

The earth makes a resolution
every 24 hours.

Rainbows are just to look at,
not to really understand.

Pine is an example of a
carnivorous tree.

Clouds are high flying fogs.

Clouds just keep circling the
earth around and around.
And around. There is not
much else to do.

Methane, a greenhouse gas,
comes from the burning
of trees and cows.

Parallel lines never meet unless
you bend one or both of them.

Music

S.O.S. is a musical term
meaning 'same only softer'.

I know what a sextet is,
but I'd rather not say.

When not working in the
church, Bach composed pieces
on a spinster in his home.

Refrain means don't do it.
A refrain in music is the part
you better not try to sing.

Stradivarius is an imaginary
prehistoric animal.

John Sebastian Bach died from
1750 to the present.

Anyone who can read all the
instrument notes at the same
time gets to be the conductor.

Handel was half German
half Italian and half English.
He was very large.

You should always say celli
when you mean there are two
or more cellos.

When electric currents go
through them, guitars
start making sounds.
So would anybody.

Question: What are kettle drums called? Answer: Kettle drums.

Question: Is the saxophone a brass or a woodwind instrument? Answer: Yes.

One semibreve equals two minions and one crochet four semi-skews.

Religion

The masculine of vixen is vicar.

Peat was made out of moses.

The result of the Reformation
was that the people could
choose either to be
Catholics or pugilists.

The Jews were a proud people, but always had trouble with unsympathetic Genitals.

Zorroastrologism was founded by Zorro. This was a duelist religion.

The seventh commandment is 'Thou shall not admit adultery'.

One of the opossums was
St Mathew he was also a taximan.

One of Jacobs sons, Joseph,
gave refuse to the Israelites.

Solomon was very fond of
animals because he had
300 porcupines.

Solomon had 300 wives
and 700 cucumbers.

David was a Hebrew king
skilled at playing the liar.
He fought with the Philatelists,
a race of people who lived
in Biblical times.

The Papal Bull was a mad bull
kept by the Pope in the Inquisition
to trample on Protestants.

Greek religion was polyphonic. Featured were gods such as Herod, Mars, and Juice.

The entire city of Constantinople rose up with a tremendous ejaculation every time the Christian Emperor Constantine came.

The Philistines are islands in the Pacific.

The message came to Abraham
that he should bear a son, and
Sarah, who was listening behind
the door, laughed.

A republican is a sinner
mentioned in the bible.

Paraffin is the next order
of angels above seraphims.

God's Own Country is Heaven.

Everyone was pleased when
Jesus healed the paralytic man,
except Simon who had to pay to
have the roof mended.

The chief missile of the Church
of England is the Prayer Book.

The end of the World will
mark a turning point
in everyone's life.

Moses received the
Ten Commandments on two
stones, and these he impressed
upon the people.

As the creator cools it hardens.

The natives of Macedonia
did not believe in Paul,
so he got stoned.

Pompeii was destroyed by an
overflow of saliva from
the Vatican.

Judyism had one big God
named 'Yahoo'.

An angry Martin Luther nailed
ninety five theocrats to
a church door.

Oliver Cromwell had a large red
nose, but under it were deeply
religious feelings.

Possession by spirits means
feeling like the devil.

R-Rated

As he walked through
his room he heard the sound
of heavy breeding.

When the wedding was over
the bridegroom clasped his
loved one tight in his arms,
while the little organ began to
swell and fill the room.

While rowing up river I
slumped over the whores in a
state of physical exhaustion.

Promiscuous behaviour leaves
them with a problem behind.

She took me indoors
and called her husband;
he was very practical
and gave me a nightdress
and some hot soup, and
told me to lie down
in his bed.

III

In the Middle Ages
people lived in mud huts with
rough mating on the floor.

The nineteenth century
was when people stopped
reproducing by hand and
started reproducing
by machine.

Madame Pompadour gained
in power while being
placed under the king.

Merchants appeared and
roamed from town to town
exposing themselves and
organizing big fairies in the
countryside.

These peace-loving animals
start their life as small,
furry balls, and they grow up
and with any luck will find a
mate, and have small, furry
balls themselves.

The Mona Liza was the most
beautiful woman ever to be
laid on canvas.

I secretly entered the boat with a feeling of suspiciousness.
I hid myself under the bed of a woman. Doing all this without the consent of the woman,
I managed to overcome my nervousness by introducing myself to her in the dark, and gained full advantage of it.

A wife should be understanding
and loving and bare
with her husband.

A census taker is man who
goes from house to house
increasing the population.

Gonads are a tribe of
wandering desert people.

Roman girls who did not marry
could become Vestigal Virgins,
a group of women who were
dedicated to burning
the internal flame.

She lay there semi-naked,
semi-conscious, and
semi-hopeful.

A gelding is a stallion who has
his tonsils taken out so he would
have more time to himself.

Early Egyptian women often
wore a garment called a calasiris.
It was a sheer dress which started
beneath the breasts which
hung to the floor.

Adolescence is the stage
between puberty and adultery.